P9-DVH-970

John Train

Comfort me with
APPLES

PHOTOGRAPHY BY
Mark E. Smith
Tristan de Terves

DISTRIBUTED BY
ANTIQUE COLLECTORS' CLUB

EASTHAMPTON, MA   WOODBRIDGE, U.K.

ACKNOWLEDGMENTS

For major research I am grateful to Maria Teresa Train, Francesca Manisco, and for editorial help, to Christine Winmill, Sara Perkins, and Jenny Gerard.

ADDITIONAL PHOTO CREDITS
Natasha Tibbott (PAGES 51, 52, 53)
John Danzer (PAGES 88–89)
Maria Bonsanti (PAGES 74–75)
Anna Rasponi (PAGE 83)
Courtesy of Farnum Hill (PAGES 92–94)

Packaging: M.T. Train

Design: Natasha Tibbott, Our Designs, Inc.

Prepress and Printing: ZoneS, Milano

© 2008 M.T. Train/Scala Books
No part of this publication may be reproduced without written permission.

ISBN 978-1-905377-27-5

Comfort me with
APPLES

From *A Month in the Country*

When I awoke, Alice Keach must have been there for some time because she was smiling. "I thought I'd find you here," she said, "when I saw you weren't with the cricketers waiting by the Shepherd. I've brought you a bag of apples. They're Ribston Pippins; they do well up here; I remember you saying you liked a firm apple."

We talked about apples. It seemed that her father had been a great apple man. In Hampshire, they'd had a fair-sized orchard planted with a wide variety and he'd brought her up to discriminate between them. "Before he bit into one, he'd sniff it, roll it around his cupped palms, then smell his hands. Then he'd tap it and finger it like a blind man. Sometimes he made me close my eyes and, when I'd had a bite, ask me to say which apple."

"You mean d'Arcy Spice or Cox's Orange?"

She laughed. "Oh no, that would have been too easy, like salt and pepper. I mean apples very much alike in shape and flavour. Like—well Cosette Reine and Coseman Reinette. I'm an apple expert. Apples are the only exam I could ever hope to pass."

—by J.L. Carr

INTRODUCTION

There is magic in apples. Perhaps it arises in part from their inviting, luminous form. Inevitably, it's Eve's *apple*, Newton's *apple*, the golden *apple*, the *apple* of discord, the *apple* of the eye, and so on. Murray's translation of the *Hippolytus of Euripides* captures it: "The apple-tree, the singing and the gold." Ornamental citrus in tubs creates a glorious effect, but an apple tree is far more beautiful than an orange tree, and has a suggestive quality and fragrance all its own. In Nordic myth you might actually make your way up to the Otherworld by climbing into the branches of an apple tree and dreaming there. And how could the lovesick girl in the Song of Solomon be comforted but with apples?

Indeed, what about this, from the old magician W.B. Yeats?

> …a glimmering girl
> With apple blossom in her hair
> Who called me by my name and ran
> And faded through the brightening air.
> Though I am old with wandering
> Through hollow lands and hilly lands,
> I will find out where she has gone,
> And kiss her lips and take her hands;
> And walk among long dappled grass,
> And pluck till time and times are done
> The silver apples of the moon,
> The golden apples of the sun.

I hope this book illuminates the beauty and utility of this most wonderful of fruits.

Apple orchards in the Trentino region of Italy.

ORIGINS

To begin at the beginning, in ancient times the more general word "fruit" was often used for what may have been the apple. Thus, the apple in Genesis, the apples thrown in the path of Atalanta, and the rest could in fact have been other fruits, but the myth-makers determined that the apple is what they would be. So the term only becomes quite exact in later times.

The apple probably originated in the Tien Shan Mountains of Kazakhstan, where a traveler describes ancient trees 60 feet tall and five feet across at the base. It flourishes in similarly cool places, notably the temperate zones. The Kazakh capital of Almaty means "father of apples." As nomadic hunter-gatherer civilizations settled down and trade among settlements began, the seeds of as many as 25 different species of apple spread along trade routes. By 8000 B.C. one or another variety existed throughout much of Europe, as has been confirmed by several archeological digs. Apple remains have been found in ancient Jericho, dating from 6500 B.C., and in the tomb of Queen Pu-A Ur in Basara, Iran, dating from 2500 B.C.

The Chinese *Precious Book of Enrichment* of 5000 B.C., tells us of a very sympathetic diplomat, Feng Li, who chose to resign his post at court in favor of pursuing his passion: fruit tree grafting. He sought to establish a business grafting apple, peach, pear, almond, and persimmon trees.

A tablet of 1500 B.C. in Mesopotamia records the sale of an apple orchard by an Assyrian, Tupkitilla, for the sum of three sheep: not an attractive price! From the same area, the law codes of the Hittites prescribe that a fine of three shekels was to be levied on anyone who allowed an apple orchard to be destroyed by fire.

In the *Odyssey*, written about 800 B.C., those excellent poets, Homer, describe an orchard:

Twelve pear trees bowing with their pendant load
And ten, that red with blushing apples glow'd.

Travel and trade throughout the ancient world brought the Greeks into contact with Persian customs and agriculture. The characteristic Persian creation of the walled and watered fruit orchard was very appealing to the Greeks. In the fifth century B.C. Xenophon, after seeing Persian walled orchards, created one of his own, and introduced into Greece the Persian word "pairidaeza," meaning both "walled garden" and paradise, which later became "paradises" in Latin and "paradise" in English.

The prodigious Greek philosopher-naturalist Theophrastos, in 300 B.C., who attracted hundreds and indeed thousands of listeners to his lectures in the Lyceum, held that understanding nature depended on identifying. He was puzzled by apples. Were they trees, which had one trunk, or shrubs, which may have several? Then as now, cultivated apples could be trained to grow with more than one trunk. Still, they were trees, he concluded, although departing from the norm in that key characteristic. He described six varieties of apples and how to cultivate them. Romans carried on his method. Cuttings (also called "scions") were taken from trees bearing good fruit and grafted onto rootstock to produce a superior apple of consistent quality. Growing from seeds produces less reliable results, although Cicero, writing in 50 B.C., encouraged citizens to save their apple seeds to help develop new species…correctly, as we see later.

Cato the Elder in *De Agricultura* from the second century B.C., also described grafting as the proper method for producing apples. In 79 A.D., Pliny the Elder identified twenty-two types of apples; to this day Roman varieties still exist.

Decorative crabapple tree in Conservatory Garden, Central Park, New York.

MY DELIGHT

The word "fruit" comes from Latin *fruor* "to delight in." The Romans esteemed the apple as beneficial to health. Galen and Hippocrates, Greek doctors living in Rome, both prescribed sweet apples to help with digestion and sour apples to avoid fainting and constipation. In addition to the health benefits, the Romans also considered the apple a luxury fruit, superior even to the fig. It was believed to be an aphrodisiac, and thus the perfect conclusion to a meal — but perhaps the evening feast rather than a business lunch. Horace, in 100 B.C., describes a delightful repast as beginning with eggs and ending with apples. The Romans even venerated a goddess, Pomona, the guardian of fruit trees.

Just as they had learned techniques of apple planting and propagating from the Persians and Greeks and went on to make it an important element of Roman civilization, so, too, as they extended their empire, the Romans brought the apple with them. When they reached England, they introduced cuttings, primarily from France, which could be grafted on the wild apple or crabapple, the one native to England.

Although systematic grafting of new species collapsed along with the Roman Empire, by then many varieties had become well established and continued to be cultivated. In 400 A.D., St. Jerome urged monks to work on grafting fruit trees "to escape sloth and the devil." Apples and recipes including apples were mentioned in many Old Saxon manuscripts, such as *The Ménagier de Paris* and the *Forme of Cury(e)*. In 1100, the apple is praised by the Salerno Medical School as helpful in treating ailments of the lungs, bowels, and nervous system. The two most commonly grown varieties in the 13th century were the Costard and the Pearmain, other varieties known at that time being the Nonpareil, the White Joaneting, and the Royal Russet.

Bartholomeus Anglicus' *Encyclopedia*, printed in 1470, is notable as one of the first printed botanical books. In the chapter on apples, he writes:

"Malus the Appyll tree is a tree yt bereth apples and is a grete tree in itself…it is more short than other trees of the wood with knottes and rinelyd Rynde. And makyth shadowe wythe thicke bowes and branches: and fayr with dyurs blossomes, and floures of swetnesse and lykynge: with goode fruyte and noble. And is gracious in sight and in taste and virtuous in medecyne…some bereth sourysh fruyte and harde, and some right soure and some right swete, with a goode savoure and mery."

In 1240, Albertus Magnus of Cologne wrote *De Vegetabilibus*, an inquiry into the natural world. In the course of this work he discusses his theory of the origin of cultivated species. By the 16th century, systematic grafting of varieties was again widely pursued in France and England. In 1618, William Lawson of Yorkshire wrote the first book in English with practical advice to gardeners wanting to grow apples, entitled *A New Orchard and Garden*. "All delight in orchards," he declared.

As Europeans began to explore the world, they brought the apple with them. It did not exist in North America before the arrival of European settlers, but the New World proved very favorable to its growth. When the Pilgrims arrived in 1620, they carried with them apple seeds (pips) rather than cuttings (scions) because the seeds were more likely to survive the voyage. When these were planted, the resulting tree pips varied somewhat from their European ancestors, differences exacerbated by subsequent exposure to American crabapple trees. In 1647, Peter Stuyvesant, governor of New Amsterdam, planted an apple tree which he had brought with him from the Netherlands. It survived until 1866, when it was accidentally destroyed. Apple trees were growing in sufficient quantity by the mid–1600s so that in 1649, Governor John Endicott of the Plymouth Colony was able to trade five hundred three-year-old trees for two hundred acres of land…a very good deal, unlike the sale by Tupkitilla. Quite a lot is known about the orchards of Louis XIV, put in place at Versailles by the royal fruitier, Jean-Baptiste de la Quintinie. The King required perfect apples throughout the year, and to that end the *Potager du Roi* grew varieties to be harvested in different seasons: the Borowitsky (favored by lovers), the Belrose Beoumoni, the Champ Gaillard, the Reinette d'Angleterre, the Fenouillet, the Pigeonnet. The French brought additional varieties to Canada, and by the early

Illustrations by the Brittish artist George Brookshaw, 1751–1823.

ABOVE: *Pomme d'Api, Carpendu de Blanc, Carpendu de Rouge, Nonsuch Apple Royal, Nonsuch Summer, Margill.*

OPPOSITE: *Phoenix Apple and Norman's Beauty.*

1700s cultivation had become widespread, and many new varieties had been created.

One hundred American varieties existed by 1800. By the 1740s, production was large enough so that apples were being shipped commercially to the West Indies. By 1872, the number of American varieties of apple had increased to more than a thousand, as listed in Downing's *Fruits and Fruit Trees in America*. Most of the varieties widely available today were already in cultivation by then, all grown from seedlings. Many of the 19th century varieties survive only as heirlooms in collectors'

orchards. Among these are the Roxbury Russet, Golden Russet, Black Gillflower, Chenango, Esopus Spitzenburg, Sweet Bough, and Winter Banana.

The apple was a staple food for American pioneers because of its versatility and preservability. It could be dried, preserved whole in cold cellars or "dry houses," or made into cider, juice, or applesauce. Later in the 19th and early 20th centuries developments in cold storage allowed commercial growers to sell the fruit throughout the year.

Cider became one of the most common uses for the apple in 18th and 19th century America. Hard cider was popular because it was easy to produce, 4% to 9% alcoholic. When that quality came to the attention of the temperance movement, commercial apple growers sought to reposition apples in the market. Thus, in 1904, the saying "An apple a day keeps the doctor away" became an advertising slogan for apples, although the health benefits of apples had been proclaimed since Roman times.

Today, the apple grows throughout the world, including all parts of Europe, Australia, New Zealand, and Chile, and in the cooler mountainous areas of Lebanon, India, Nepal, China, and Japan. The largest producers are China, Italy and France, and within the United States, the states of Washington, Michigan, and New York.

As the fruit became widely cultivated in Europe and America, the tradition of giving apples to teachers arose. Teachers were poorly paid, and their compensation consisted partly of food sent by pupils' parents. Apples, which were abundant, were given to teachers by the bushel. Then, as the teachers' pay rose, the gift of an apple to the teacher became more symbolic than practical.

Apples in a basket. Roman mosaic in the Bardo museum, Tunisia.

BELOW: *Apples in a glass jar. Fresco from the house of Julia Felix, Pompeii.*

OPPOSITE: *Mural frescos depicting apple trees. Detail from a wall of the Villa di Livia, Villa Farnesina, Rome.*

QUINCE.
CYDONIA VULGARIS.

APPLE.

APPLE.

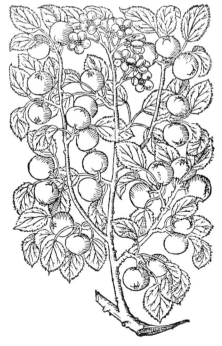

"CHOKING LEAN CRAB-TREE"

APPLE-TREE.

OPPOSITE ABOVE: *Quince and Apple block prints, Venice, 1554.* OPPOSITE BELOW LEFT: *Apple, block print, Antwerp, 1581.* OPPOSITE BELOW RIGHT: *"Choking Lean Crab-Tree," block print, London, 1597.*

Apple tree, earliest known copperplate etching, Frankfurt, 1590.

Poma flore multiplici.

Print from the Besler Florigenium *depicting a double flowered apple.*

Print of a pear-shaped apple branch by the British botanist William Hooker, 1785–1865.

Fleurs de Pommier. *Illustration of apple blossom, by the French botanist/artist*
Pierre Joseph Redouté, 1759–1840.

JOHNNY APPLESEED

The spread of the apple in America was helped along by a strange but real man named John Chapman, whimsically styled "Johnny Appleseed." He is probably the most famous person specifically associated with this fruit. He was born in Leominster, Massachusetts, on September 26, 1774, and probably died in Fort Wayne, Indiana, on March 18, 1845. In 1800, he set out to explore the country, in order to spread the principles of Swedenborgian philosophy, and to plant apple trees everywhere, in the hope that no one need go hungry. He traveled barefoot, sometimes, it is believed, wearing a saucepan for a hat, and living on a vegetarian diet of buttermilk and "beebread" (pollen). He planted trees of the Jonathan variety and established nurseries in New York, Pennsylvania, Ohio, Illinois, Kentucky, and Indiana, some of which still exist and bear fruit. He became an extremely famous, well-loved figure, and the subject of many legends and songs.

Edgar Lee Masters, of the *Spoon River Anthologies*, wrote a poem about him:

JOHNNY APPLESEED

When the air of October is sweet and cold as the wine of apples
Hanging ungathered in frosted orchards along the Grand River,
I take the road that winds by the resting fields and wander
From Eastmanville to Nuncia down to the Villa Crossing.

I look for old men to talk with, men as old as the orchards,
Men to tell me of ancient days, of those who built and planted,
Lichen gray, branch broken, bent and sighing,
Hobbling for warmth in the sun and for places to sit and smoke.

For there is a legend here, a tale of the croaking old ones
That Johnny Appleseed came here,
Planted some orchards around here,
When nothing was here but the pine trees, oaks and the beeches,
And nothing was here but the marshes, lake and the river.

Peter Van Zylen is ninety and this he tells me:
My father talked with Johnny Appleseed there on the hill-side,
There by the road on the way to Fruitport, saw him
Clearing pines and oaks for a place for an apple orchard.
Peter Van Zylen says: He got that name from the people
For carrying apple-seed with him and planting orchards
All the way from Ohio, through Indiana across here,
Planting orchards, they say, as far as Illinois.

Johnny Apple said, so my father told me
I go to a place forgotten, the orchards will thrive and be here
For children to come, who will gather and eat hereafter.
And few will know who planted, and none will understand.

I laugh, said Johnny Appleseed: Some fellow buys this timber
Five years, perhaps from to-day, begins to clear for barley.
And here in the midst of the timber is hidden an apple orchard.
How did it come here? Lord! Who was it here before me?

Yes, I was here before him, to make these places of worship,
Labor and laughter and gain in the late October.
Why did I do it, eh? Some folks say I am crazy.
Where do my labors end? Far west, God only knows!

Said Johnny Appleseed there on the hill-side: Listen!
Beware of the deceit of nurseries, sellers of seeds of the apple.
Think! You labor for years in trees not worth the raising.
You planted what you knew not, bitter or sour for sweet.

No luck more bitter than poor seed, but one as bitter:
The planting of perfect seed in soil that feeds and fails,
Nourishes for a little, and then goes spent forever.
Look to your seed, he said, and remember the soil.

MYTH RELIGION AND ART

Middle Ages Herbarium,
Domus Viridiana.

THE BIBLE STORY

The Tree of the Knowledge of Good and Evil is described in Genesis as "good for food and pleasant to the eyes, and a tree to be desired to make one wise." However, in Biblical times the apple tree did not grow in the Middle East, so as mentioned earlier the reference may be to something else—the apricot, peach, fig, or pomegranate. Other identifications are the quince, grape, citron, wheat, or carob. The identification of the Tree of the Knowledge of Good and Evil as an apple probably arose when Christianity reached the Teutonic people of Western Europe, who worshipped a mother earth-goddess, whose symbol was an apple. In that context, the apple carried the meaning of love, knowledge and immortality, and could thus be identified as the fruit consumed by Adam and Eve. In any event, the Garden of Eden is mythical, so we can furnish it with apples if we so desire.

The Fall of Adam and Eve, *detail of bas-relief by Federico Lelli, Church of St. Petronio, Bologna.*

The apple had a number of qualities which made it an appropriate symbol of temptation in that story: The rounded shape indicated fertility, and the sweet taste, desire. The most likely alternative fruit of the Tree of the Knowledge of Good and Evil would be the fig, greatly esteemed in the eastern Mediterranean, and whose shape has erotic overtones. The Latin word for apple is "malum," which also means "evil," and so perhaps helped influence the choice of the specific fruit in the Genesis story.

In western European art, particularly that of France and Germany, Adam and Eve ordinarily appear in the Garden of Eden with an apple tree by the 13th century, although sometimes a fig tree. Italian and Byzantine artists were likely to prefer the fig to the apple. Milton's *Areopagitica* in 1644 identified the fruit of the Tree of the Knowledge of Good and Evil as an apple, which pretty well settled the issue. In the Islamic tradition, however, the olive or fig continued to be the fruit of the Tree, although in the writings of a secret Islamic sect in 900 the prophet Muhammad attains eternal life by inhaling the scent of an apple brought to him by an angel.

The Song of Solomon presents a fruit, perhaps the apple, in a slightly different guise. There, the apple, or possibly the quince, is associated with the female breast and its association with desire, sweetness, love and marriage.

Egyptian Jewish women sought to give birth beneath apple trees.

Ottoman Jewish woman placed apples on their heads when about to give birth.*

---

* Similarly, in China, women about to give birth appealed to a fertility goddess, who appeared to them in a dream, giving an apple or peach to the mother of a boy and a plum or a pear to the mother of a girl.

The Hesperides. *Detail of triptych wooden panel by the German painter Hans von Marees, 1837–1887.*

THE APPLES OF THE HESPERIDES

In Greek myth, at the marriage of Zeus, the king of the gods, with Hera, the earth-goddess, Gaia, gives her a fruit tree as a wedding present. Hera keeps it, or possibly an entire grove of them, in a walled orchard in the west, the Garden of the Hesperides. These were nymphs, daughters of a titan, Atlas, who on his shoulders held up the earth and the sky. Hera had also given the trees a special guardian, the dragon Ladon, who having a hundred heads, would always be vigilant. The trees justified such care because the golden fruit they bore bestowed immortality.

Married or not, Zeus copulated with all and sundry, to his wife's great vexation. Many offspring resulted. One was Hercules. He survived Hera's vengeful designs against him during his youth, but after he married and had children, Hera caused him to lose his mind and kill his wife and offspring: about the limit in persecution by a jealous spouse. When Hercules returned to his senses, he was horrified and anxious to redeem himself. Apollo's oracle told him to serve Eurystheus, King of Tiryns and Mycenae, for twelve years as punishment. During those years, Hercules performed the famous Twelve Labors.

For the eleventh, Eurystheus commanded Hercules to bring him the golden apples (or oranges, or whatever they were) from the Garden of the Hesperides. Hercules captured a sea-god, Nereus, who knew the location of the garden. In the meanwhile, Prometheus had betrayed the gods by selling the secret of fire, and as punishment had been condemned to eternal torment: He was chained to a rock, where an eagle came to eat his liver every day. Hercules rescued him, killing the eagle. To express his thanks, Prometheus hatched a plan for him to steal the apples. At Prometheus' suggestion, Hercules offered to hold up the sky for Atlas while Atlas recovered the apples from his daughters, the Hesperides. When Atlas returned with the apples, Hercules tricked him into resuming his burden, and then went to present the apples to Eurystheus. In the end, though, since the apples were ultimately the property of the gods, they were returned to the Garden by Athena.

The Judgement of Paris. *Painting on wood by the German painter Lucas Cranach the Elder, 1472 – 1553.*

Pomona, *guardian of fruit trees. Illustration by the British artist Sir Edward Burne-Jones, 1833–1898.*

Golden apples appear as a divine gift in another Greek myth. Atalanta was the courageous, adventurous, athletically-gifted daughter of a man who had wished for a son. She accomplished many feats with male companions, but to his vexation chose not to marry. Atalanta eventually made a deal with her father: She undertook to marry the man who could beat her in a foot-race. She beat them all until Hippomenes (also called Melanion) used a trick suggested to him by Aphrodite. He brings three golden apples with him, and three times, as the race progresses, he tosses a golden apple near Atalanta's feet. Each time she pauses to retrieve it, and he gains on her. As she picks up the last one, Hippomenes springs over the finish line and claims her as his bride. (Later, though, Aphrodite, or possibly Zeus, turned them both into lions.) Pursuant to this story the ancient Greeks held that a man could propose marriage to a woman by tossing her an apple. If she caught it, she was accepting him.

In another tale, Zeus gives a banquet to celebrate the marriage of the goddess Thetis to King Peleus. Eris, the goddess of discord and chaos, is not invited. She appears anyway, and bowls into the gathering of gods and humans a golden apple inscribed with a "K," meaning "Kallisti" or "for the fairest." It is immediately claimed by three goddesses, Hera, Athena, and Aphrodite, who appeal to Zeus to choose among them. Preferring to stay out of trouble, he refuses, and sends them instead to Prince Paris of Troy. Each goddess tries to bribe him: Hera by offering him power, Athena wisdom, and Aphrodite the love of the most beautiful woman in the world. Paris awards the apple to Aphrodite, and in return receives Helen, the most beautiful of all, with whom he returns home to Troy. But Helen is already married to King Menelaus. The outrage of the Greeks brings on the Trojan War, and eventually Troy's utter destruction.

In yet another story, Gervasius, writing of the conquests of Alexander the Great, describes Alexander's quest for the "water of life" in India. He meets priests there who ate special apples which allowed them to live to be four hundred years old.

NORSE MYTHOLOGY

The goddess Idunn keeps apples which she gives as food to the gods to render them both immortal and forever young. However, the god Loki is snatched up by an eagle when on a trip with his fellow gods Thor and Odin. The eagle promises to let Loki go on condition that Loki bring him Idunn to marry and thus let him gain eternal youth. When the gods notice what has happened they threaten Loki with death, and he restores Idunn and her apples back to them. The myth holds that the gods will remain young by eating apples until the "ragna rok," the end of the current age of the world.

In Norse tradition, apples were the embodiment not only of long life, but also of wisdom and love. Wands of apple wood were used in Norse love rituals. An echo of these rituals perhaps survives in the traditional Danish belief that apples will wither in the presence of adulterers.

In a related tradition from ancient Silesia (now part of Poland), a maiden who sleeps with an apple under her pillow on New Year's Eve will dream of her future husband. And in the folklore of several other cultures, a maiden who peels an apple and throws the peel over her shoulder will discover the initials of her husband-to-be.

The Norse goddess Idunn, is the keeper of the apples of youth, which keep the gods young and strong. She is pictured with her husband Braga the wise, the god of the poetic art.

Ladies sitting in an orchard. Engraving, 19th century.

Apples are deeply involved in the rituals and beliefs of British and Celtic folklore. These beliefs encompass many aspects of the apple: as a means to eternal youth, as a magical food, and as an element of prophecy. The apple tree is one of the trees of the Otherworld, and along with the oak considered the most noble.

The Celtic Isle of Avalon, part of the Otherworld, also called "the Orchard," or Avallach, meaning the Isle of Apples, was the land of kings and heroes and of fairies and magic. The wounded King Arthur is taken there by his sister Morgan le Fay, the Queen of the Fairies and the ruler of the Isle. She heals him, and waits until his return to free the Welsh and Cornish from their conquerors. In the meantime, the apples of the Isle of Avalon provide its inhabitants with the food of youth and health. In a related Celtic practice, apples were occasionally buried with the dead to feed them in the next world.

The magical and youth-giving properties of the apple combine in the medieval Irish story of Prince Connla the Fair. He glimpses a beautiful fairy sailing near the shore in a crystal boat. She offers him an apple from the world of the fairies. After he takes a bite, he becomes forever hers. They live on her island among apple trees, which provide them with food for an eternity without winter. Apple trees like these were also believed to heal deeper spiritual ills. So in ancient times the Irish declared the cutting down of an apple tree a crime punishable by death.

The apple figures in ancient Druidic traditions and rituals. The symbol which the Druids considered most holy was the Three Rays of Light, which represented the three apples of the Tree of Knowledge. Druids sought to enter the Otherworld through magical rituals. One was by using the Silver Bough, created by wrapping silver apple-shaped bells around a branch from a magical apple tree. When it was shaken, the sound would induce a trance that allowed the listener to enter the Otherworld.

The Druid tale most closely associated with the Silver Bough is the story of the Voyage of Bran. An Otherworld woman approaches Bran and entices him with a Silver Bough. Enchanted, he follows her across the seas and into the Otherworld, where he has many adventures.

Druid bards and shamans (or ovates) used apple branches wrapped in bells of bronze, silver, or gold as symbols of their positions. The ability of the bell-wrapped apple bough to induce a trance state in the listener relates, it has been suggested, to the properties of hard cider. The Druid magician Merlin lived and taught in a grove of apple trees, where he also received a magic apple from the Fairy Queen, which gave him the gift of prophecy. When Merlin later had a fit of madness, he took refuge under an apple tree.

This trance state leading to prophecy or folly, which could be induced by apple eating or drinking, could lead to more sinister developments. One appears in the medieval tale of Snow White, whom the evil Queen, using a poisoned apple, puts into an eternal sleep. In the 13th century, Thomas the Rhymer of Scotland was warned against eating an apple offered to him by the Fairy Queen. Once he had partaken of it, he would be unable to remain in the mortal world.

In the Druid tradition, the apple, in remembrance of those inhabiting the Isle of Apples, is one of the foods included in the ritual of the Dumb Supper, celebrated on the Day of the Apple, or Samhain (Halloween) Eve. Dinner is served and eaten in silence, with a place at the table set for the dead. Servers with broken crockery walk backwards and never glance at that place. At the conclusion of the meal, the uneaten food and the broken dishes are taken to the woods and given to the spirits of the dead - the Pookas. In a related observance, all the apples left on trees after Samhain are not harvested, but are left to nourish the dead.

Sculpture on left depicting Eve from the St. Lorenz Church in Nuremberg, Germany.

Original Sin *and* The Lord Reproaches Adam and Eve, *from the Visconti Hours by Giovannino dei Grassi, late 14th century.*

The Fall. *Earthenware dish, English 1635,*

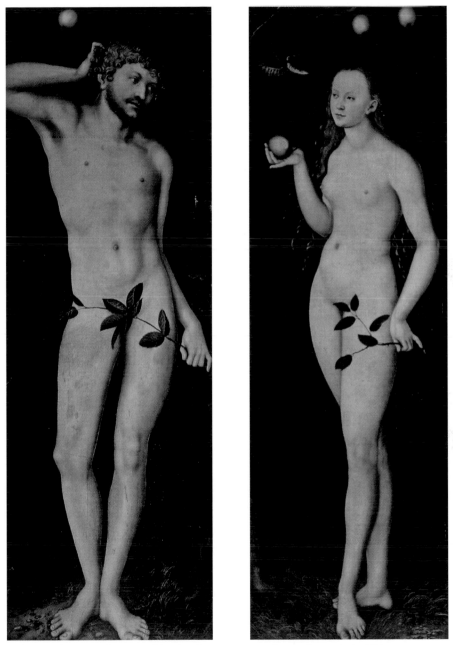

Adam and Eve. *Oil on panel by the German painter Lucas Cranach the Elder, 1472–1553.*

Madonna and Child under an Apple Tree. *Oil on canvas by the German painter Lucas Cranach the Elder, 1472–1553.*

Cupid complaining to Venus. *Oil on canvas by the German painter
Lucas Cranach the Elder, 1472–1553.*

The Garden of Eden with the Fall of Man. *Oil Panel by the Flemish painter Jan Brueghel the Elder, 1568–1625.*

Detail from Adam and Eve. *Oil painting, French School, XVIth century.*

Detail from Flora. *Oil on canvas by the Flemish painter Frans Ykens, 1601–1693.*

Detail from an oil painting by Dutch painter Gerard ter Borch, 1617–1681.

Detail from Apples. *Oil on canvas by French painter Paul Cézanne, 1839–1906.*

Still life with Apples and a Pomegranate. *Oil on canvas by French painter Gustave Courbet, 1819–1877.*

Detail from Still Life with Flowers and Fruits. *Oil on canvas by the Spanish painter Juan van der Hamen y Leon, 1596–1631.*

OPPOSITE: The Apple Tree. *Oil on canvas by Norwegian painter Edward Munch, 1863–1944.*

ABOVE: Apple Harvest. *Watercolor by Swedish artist Carl Larsson, 1853–1919.*

BELOW: Apple Tree in Sweden. *Oil on canvas by Swedish painter Gunvor Hellström, 1909–1976.*

FORBIDDEN FRUIT

The apple is riddled with symbolism. If you cut one in half along the equator, so to speak, the arrangement of the compartments containing the pips forms a five-pointed star, a pentagram. This shape is considered to represent the spiritual aspect of man, so the pentagram within the whole fruit is considered to represent his spiritual combined with his physical aspects.

Then, the spheroid shape of the fruit has given rise to a variety of interpretations. Origen held the apple to be the "image of the richness, sweetness and savor of the Word of God." But the round shape of the apple is also interpreted as a symbol of earthy desires, which we are warned against. In this interpretation, the apple becomes the symbol of man's awareness that he may follow either his own desires or the word of God. He must then make the choice of turning toward either the earthly or the divine.

Roman emperors carried a golden apple in their hand, a model of the terrestrial globe, thus signifying earthly power.

The apple appears as a symbol in literature, art and even music, sometimes with a sinister aspect. In Latin, the words for apple (*malus*) and "evil" (*malum*) are similar in the singular and identical in the plural (*mala*).

Perhaps this is why it is the forbidden fruit in the story of Adam and Eve. When Eve persuades Adam to partake, it became a symbol for temptation, the fall of humankind into sin, and finally sin itself.

The visible projection of the larynx at the front of the neck is called the Adam's apple, on the theory that a piece of the forbidden fruit was stuck in Adam's throat.

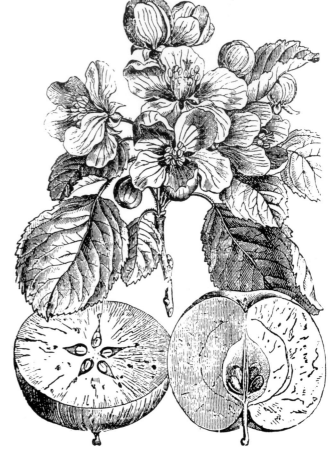

Apple blossom and fruit, engraving, 19ᵗʰ century.

Of course, the apple does not always embody this negative symbolism. For example, there are several references to "the apple of your eye" (Deuteronomy 32:10; Psalms 17:8; Proverbs 7:2 and Zechariah 2:8), implying that a person or object is held in great esteem. A verse in Proverbs (25:11) says that "a word fitly spoken is like apples of gold." In the Song of Solomon, the apple becomes a symbol of beauty, and is used in a sensual context. In Joel (1:12), the intense feeling of lost joy is compared to the withering away of an apple tree.

The apple is also a prominent motif in many Russian and European fairy tales, which often involve the theft of golden apples from a king, usually by a bird, with deplorable consequences. Among these are *Tsarevitch Ivan, the Fire Bird and the Grey Wolf* (Russian); *The Golden Bird* and *The Golden Mermaid*, both German; and *The Nine Peahens and the Golden Apples* (Bulgarian). In the Romanian tale *Prâslea the Brave and the Golden Apples*, a fantastic creature called a zmeu steals the golden apples.

In the German fairy tale, *Snow White*, the magical apple is not golden but red and poisonous.

Twentieth century engraving depicting boys playing in an apple tree.

Illustration for children's book by Elsa Beskow.

Mid 20th century children's alphabet book depicting typical apple image used for letter "A."

In the William Tell story, that champion of the Swiss in the struggle for independence from Austria splits an apple on the head of his son with a well-placed arrow. The feat probably has no foundation in fact, but the legend inspired Schiller's play *Wilhelm Tell* (1804), which in turn was the basis for Rossini's opera *Guillaume Tell* (1829).

Apples are an important element in Richard Wagner's *Das Rheingold*, the first of the four operas in *Der Ring des Nibelungen*, first produced in Munich in 1869. Central to a convoluted plot involving giants, gods and a dwarf, is Freia, the goddess who cultivates golden apples that give eternal youth. When she is kidnapped by the giants Fafner and Fasolt, the gods, lacking access to the magical apples, grow old and weak.

Poets in times both ancient and modern, have invoked apples in their work. In the seventh century B.C. Sappho wrote,

> Art thou the topmost apple
> The gatherers could not reach,
> Reddening on the bough?

William Tell shooting the apple from his son's head, engraving 1698.

In scenes from the New Testament, the apple evolves into a symbol of redemption. It is often grasped by the Christ child, confirming that he is the "new Adam" and has assumed his mission to redeem humanity.

In another painting inspired by the Bible — Caravaggio's *The Supper at Emmaus* — a fruit basket containing a rotten apple and other decaying fruits sits on the table, a symbolic reference to original sin.

Artists also make use of the apple as a symbol of love and sexuality in secular paintings. The Belgian Surrealist René Magritte painted a famous witty and somewhat disturbing picture of a man in a suit and bowler hat whose face is obscured by a green apple.

Apple Charlotte, a dessert, consists of sautéed, spiced apples in a shell of buttered bread, and memorializes Charlotte Buff in Goethe's 1774 novel, *The Sorrows of Young Werther*. Unfortunately, in the novel Charlotte's suitor, Werther, is a hopelessly vague, distracted and romantic youth, who eventually shoots himself. The distressing tale inspired many suicides among sad young romantics of the period. On the other hand, other authorities hold that the Charlotte of the dish was Queen Charlotte, wife of George III, a keen supporter of apple growers.

In folk art the fruit itself is used to make such creations as the apple-head doll. Good examples of early ones are sought by collectors and new ones are shown at craft festivals. To construct an apple doll, you begin by peeling a large apple. Leave some skin at the top and bottom to make sure it retains its round shape. Carve the eyes far apart, to allow for shrinkage as the apple dries. (Or after the apple has dried you can define facial features with objects such as cloves or beads.) Stick a dowel into the cored bottom and let it dry for three to four weeks. Create hair with yarn or cotton and use wire and cloth to form the body. Then dress the apple-face doll with imagination.

Snow White, *illustration for children's album by Cristina Cini.*

WASSAIL

Several ancient Celtic and British traditions associated with the apple persist in slightly altered form today. In November, the Druids celebrated the Day of the Apple—La Mas Ushal or La Mas Nbhal—with a concoction mixed in a recipe that is now identified as the Wassail Bowl, which included cooked crabapples, cider or ale, honey, brown sugar, cinnamon, nutmeg, and cloves. The key ingredient, a roasted crabapple, is mentioned by Shakespeare:

> And sometimes lurk I in a gossip's bowl
> In very likeness of a roasted Crab.

…spoken by Puck in *Midsummer Night's Dream*. Bobbing for apples in a tub of water, which still marks an observance of Halloween, was an ancient Scottish and Irish tradition, along with biting apples swinging from strings.

Wassailing (derived from Anglo Saxon "wes hal," good health) started on an autumnal Day of the Apple, and migrated to a winter ceremony, still apple-related. A further adaptation has brought wassailing to Christmastime. In Great Britain it became the custom to wassail the oldest tree in the orchard, known as Apple Tree Man, on Twelfth Night, to protect the tree from evil spirits during the winter and let it produce a bountiful harvest in the spring. In a variation, all the trees that had produced satisfying harvests of apples were honored with wassailing; those that had disappointed were ignored. The poet Herrick elaborated on this convention in his *Ceremonies of Christmas Eve:*

> Wassaile the trees, that they may beare
> You many a Plum and many a Peare:
> For more or less fruits they will bring,
> As you do give them Wassailing.

The ceremony of wassailing begins with the family and farm workers going out to the orchard after supper. Bits of toast soaked in cider are placed in the branches of the trees to be honored. These are intended for the robins, the spirits of the trees. The company then toasts the tree with warm apple cider, into which roasted apples are mixed. Here is an example:

> Here's to thee, old apple-tree!
> Whence thou may'st bud, and whence thou may'st blow,
> Bushel—bushel-bags full!
> And my pockets full too! Huzza!

Finally, some of the warm cider and apples are either flung into the branches or poured on the roots. The celebration concludes with women and children shouting, and gunshots from the men to chase away evil spirits.

A TRADITIONAL GLOUCESTERSHIRE WASSAIL SONG

> Wassail! wassail! all over the town,
> Our toast is white and our ale it is brown;
> Our bowl it is made of the white apple tree;
> With the wassailing bowl we'll drink to thee.
>
> Here's to our horse, and to his right ear,
> God send our master a happy new year;
> A happy new year as e'er he did see,
> With my wassailing bowl I drink to thee.
>
> So here is to Cherry and to his right cheek
> Pray God send our master a good piece of beef
> And a good piece of beef that may we all see
> With the wassailing bowl, we'll drink to thee.

Here's to our mare, and to her right eye,
God send our mistress a good Christmas pie;
A good Christmas pie as e'er I did see,
With my wassailing bowl I drink to thee.

So here's to Broad Mary and to her broad horn
May God send our master a good crop of corn
And a good crop of corn that may we all see
With the wassailing bowl, we'll drink to thee.

And here is to Fillpail and to her left ear
Pray God send our master a happy New Year
And a happy New Year as e'er he did see
With the wassailing bowl, we'll drink to thee.

Here's to our cow, and to her long tail,
God send our master us never may fail
Of a cup of good beer; I pray you draw near,
And our jolly wassail it's then you shall hear.

Come butler, come fill us a bowl of the best
Then we hope that your soul in heaven may rest
But if you do draw us a bowl of the small
Then down shall go butler, bowl and all.

Be here any maids? I suppose here be some;
Sure they will not let young men stand on the cold stone!
Sing hey O, maids! Come trole back the pin,
And the fairest maid in the house let us all in.

Then here's to the maid in the lily white smock
Who tripped to the door and slipped back the lock
Who tripped to the door and pulled back the pin
For to let these jolly wassailers in.

Contemporary superstition continues to link apples with magic and prophecy. The apple itself and the pentagram concealed inside it are both considered protective symbols, and the tree is an element in several magical practices. Amulets are tied into bags and hung in the branches of apple trees in order to bring the practitioner love, health, prosperity, or another wish. The most powerful place to practice magic is under a blooming apple tree, in order to involve the scent of the apple in the ritual.

Wands made from apple-wood trees are believed to be most powerful when used in rituals involving deities associated with apples. They may be used when you call upon Morgan le Fay, the Queen of the Fairies and the ruler of Avalon, or if you want to summon a spirit that inhabits Avalon.

Climbing into an apple tree has been held to be a way to approach the source of many of the myths associated with the magic of the apple, as well as a way to see into the future.

And well do I remember the charming song, "Don't sit under the apple tree/With anyone else but me/Anyone else but me/Anyone else but me…"

Apple blossom in the Valley of Ourika, Morocco.

AN APPLE A DAY

The adage, "An apple a day keeps the doctor away,"* whose first known occurrence is only at the beginning of the 20th century, is a way of saying that apples prevent both constipation *and* diarrhea. A miracle! An old Pembrokeshire proverb claims, "To eat an apple before going to bed, will make the doctor beg for his bread." A fresh apple makes a good snack: easy to carry, flavorful, filling, and only 90 calories. The average apple is from 80 to 85% water and 6% to 10% or so sugar, with very little protein or fat.

The apple also acts as a natural toothbrush, as not only do its juices cleanse the teeth but its hardness stimulates the gums.

It's best not to peel the fruit, which removes the most beneficial nutrients, but the trees may be sprayed with pesticides, so do wash it before eating.

The apple's fiber content is partly insoluble—which keeps the bowels in good working order and may thus lower the risk of colon cancer—and partly soluble, notably the pectin, the ingredient used to thicken jams and jellies, which lowers blood cholesterol levels. It forms a gel which slows the rise in blood sugar in diabetics.

In addition to small amounts of vitamins A and C, an apple contains potassium, which may reduce the risk of stroke, and boron, a trace element believed to strengthen bones against osteoporosis.

Chang Y. Lee, a professor of food science and technology at Cornell, and his researchers have used Red Delicious apples from New York State to study how their naturally occurring antioxidants can protect the brain from such neurodegenerative diseases as Parkinson's and Alzheimer's.

The apple peeler. *Oil painting by Dutch painter Gabriel Metsu, 1629–1669.*

APPLE CIDER VINEGAR

Some attribute to apple cider vinegar an exceptional healing power. Cheap and readily available, it may help control weight, improve digestion, relieve pain and itchiness when rubbed on insect bites, and even control dandruff. It contains the same nutrients as apples—pectin, potassium, and beta-carotene—plus the enzymes and amino acids formed in the fermentation process.

Sore eyes may be treated with a poultice of mashed rotten apples. According to Scottish herbalist Mary Beith, whooping cough can be relieved by a concoction of apples and rowanberries, sweetened with brown sugar. Observing that the bacillus of typhoid fever cannot long survive in apple juice, she recommended treating unclean drinking water with apple cider.

Researchers at Yale have demonstrated the relaxing power of whiffing a mug of mulled apple cider. Details of cider making are on pages 92–93.

---

* "Particularly if you throw it at him hard enough," goes the continuation.

COOKING

Woman Peeling Apples. *Oil painting by Dutch painter Gerard ter Borch, 1617–1681.*

Apples grow in summer, are harvested in autumn, and can be stored over the winter. Apples without bruises or breaks in the skin can be stored whole in a cool, dry space. They must be completely intact, since a bruise or split in the peel allows the release of an enzyme that causes decay. They mustn't touch each other, so that any decay will not migrate among them.

How should one store apples until you want to eat them? In the open air they dry out and lose their firm texture. So keep them in the refrigerator. Then, when you're ready, put them out at room temperature until the aroma returns. You may wait a day or two or more.

Most wild apples are so sour that as Thoreau said, they would set a squirrel's teeth on edge. One theory of how some sweet apples evolved is thanks to Kazakhstan's bears. Like humans, they prefer sweet fruit, so in good years, according to this idea, bears gorge on sweet fruit, and distribute the seeds intact over wide areas, accompanied by dollops of manure—a prime fertilizer.

Pliny the Elder, in the first century A.D., further specifies a cool, dry storage space with circulating air and a window facing away from the sun.

The fruit has been dried in many different ways over the centuries. Medieval Europeans peeled and cored them and then strung them whole on long cords in airy and warm drying rooms. Later the apples were cut crosswise into rings before being strung up. This method produced more dependable results, since the rings would dry more quickly than the whole apples, making them less likely to decay.

Earlier centuries have favored other methods. Norfolk liked "biffins." An apple is placed whole and with the peel intact in a warm oven. It gradually shrivels and is preserved by the partial cooking process. The result is rather like a red prune. The biffins are then packed closely together to last through the winter.

In the Loire Valley the locals used a similar technique to produce "*pommes tapées*." The fruits are peeled before being placed in an oven. Over the course of five days, while gradually cooking, they are tapped occasionally with a mallet. This produces a flattened shape that can be easily stored, and then soaked in red wine before eating.

You can also preserve apples by converting them into apple butter. Fruits that have already been puréed by being boiled are then further cooked with cider until a very concentrated liquid results. The Dutch brought this practice to the new world, where it is now an American specialty.

Preserving apples became much easier when cold storage became available in the 20th century. Carbon dioxide storage is now also used, which much delays spoilage because unlike oxygen, carbon dioxide is not part of the chemical process that leads to spoilage.

Just as methods of storing apples were developed in centuries past and remained in use for years, the basic ways of cooking and consuming apples were established centuries ago. Apples lend themselves easily to consumption in cooked or fresh form. In some parts of the world, they are clearly divided into eating and cooking varieties, although others make no such distinction.

The British are particularly clear in categorizing apples as either being for eating or for cooking. The latter when cooked readily reduce to purée. They fall into two general categories: the early-ripening apples of the Godlin type, which are green-skinned and soft and exemplified by the Grenadier, or the late-ripening Lena's Prince Albert type, which are red-striped and exemplified by the Bramley. The British custom during the Victorian and Edwardian times of drinking port with dessert led to a preference for apples with a "nutty" flavor, considered a good accompaniment.

While the British eat imported Red and Golden Delicious apples, their preference is for the Coxes and the Russets, although the peculiar look of the Russet seems to have limited its appeal. Americans make few distinctions between eating and cooking apples, using most varieties for either.

Appearance is important to Americans, with red the preferred color. The red Rome Beauty seems to appeal primarily by its appearance rather than flavor. The Golden Delicious is also popular.

The most basic way to cook an apple is to roast it. This was accomplished in ancient times by holding the whole apple on a stick pointed toward the fire.* In order to roast the apple more evenly, various elaborate racks have been devised, with metal backs to reflect the heat back onto the fruit. The baked apple has a very long history in English cooking. Piers Ploughman describes "all the povere peple" with "baken apples broghte in his lappes." The combination of a roasted apple with caraway seeds is a centuries-old English recipe. As Passage notes in the *Booke of Nurture*, "After mete pepyns, caraway in comfits." In Shakespeare's *Henry IV*, Shallow offers Falstaff "a pippin and a dish of caraway." The tradition of eating roast apples with caraway continues at Trinity College, Cambridge, and at some London Livery company dinners.

In classical times, Apicius recorded a recipe for apples cooked with diced pork. The tang of the apple counterbalances the fat of the meat. Similarly, the combination of apple and herring, a fatty fish, has for centuries been popular in Scandinavia and Northern Europe. A modern dish in this old tradition is mutton baked with apples and onions. The salted meat, with extra fat trimmed, is put in a baking dish and covered with chopped onions and sliced tart apples and baked until tender.

The apple combined with pastry accounts for the most familiar of apple recipes and a wide array of regional variations. Our familiar apple pie is completely encased in crust. This technique is descended from the medieval "raised pie." Other examples are the British pork pie and the French "pâté en croûte." In medieval recipes sweet or savoury fillings, were encased in pastry "coffyns."

The apple pie now plays a prominent symbolic role in American lore. In 19th century rural America, pie was frequently served as breakfast food, since it provided a hearty start to the day. Stephen Vincent Benet's *The Devil and Daniel Webster* ends with the great man telling his client, "I hope there's pie for breakfast, Neighbor Stone."

The current-day British apple pie is made in a deep dish, with the crust only on the top, a form that first appeared in the 17th century. In the traditional British apple pie recipe, verjuice (a crabapple extract) is added for its tartness, and quinces for further tartness and to give a pink tinge to the pie. Cinnamon and ginger are sometimes added, as is saffron, for color.

---

* My mother used to try this late in the season when we were still in Maine. The product resembled a black golf ball.

Baked apples with prunes, apricots and almonds.

Small apple tart, danish apple bread, apple muffins and an apple crumb loaf.

Dried apples.

McIntosh sliced and cut apple.

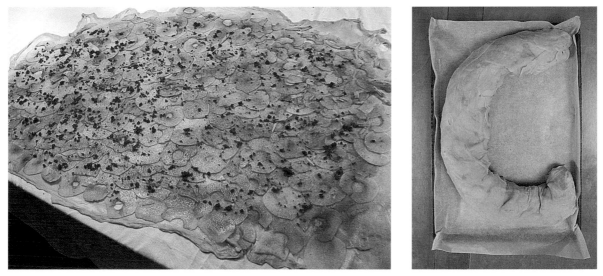

Apple strudel dough stretched on table cloth with apple slices ready to roll. RIGHT: *Strudel ready for baking.*

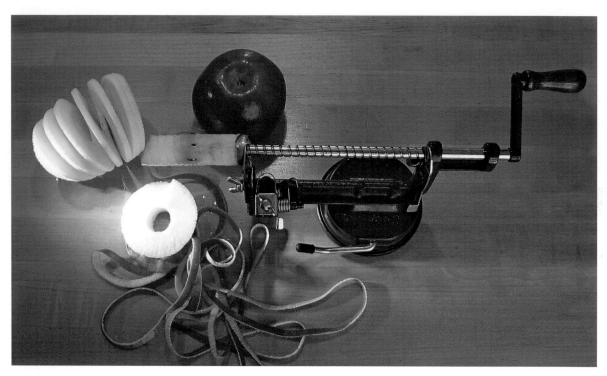

Peel Away lathe-type apple peeling and coring machine. *A modern reproduction of one of the first mass-produced kitchen appliances, the first patents for which appeared as early as 1803.*

Apple pie.

Ingredients for Waldorf Salad: *apples, celery, walnuts, mayonnaise.*

OPPOSITE: Waldorf Salad *on a bed of lettuce. A Christmas decoration: a piglet with an apple in his mouth.*

The French variation of this dish is the excellent "*tarte aux pommes*," made with the pastry underneath the fruit. The apples, selected for their ability to hold their shape when cooked, are sliced thinly and carefully arranged in a pleasing pattern on the pastry before baking. After baking, they are topped with a layer of apple jelly.

The German recipes for apples in pastry are the *Apfeltorte* and *Apfelstrudel*. These both surround the apples with pastry. Their recipes are closely related to the apple dumpling recipes of Britain and Northern Europe. They originally called for the apple to be boiled in traditional dumpling-making style. In the middle of the 19th century, however, a new practice arose. The apple was peeled, cored, stuffed with a mixture of butter, sugar, and spices, wrapped in a pastry crust, and then baked, rather than boiled. This became the common practice, although the inaccurate term "dumpling" was retained.

Americans commonly eat apple pie with ice cream, while the British favor cream or cheese.

Apples can also be baked into cakes. In England, particularly in the southwest, the traditional recipe calls for chopped raw apples to be added to the cake mixture. Swedish applecakes are more akin to puddings, made with alternating layers of apple purée and spiced breadcrumbs. This preparation is similar to ones known elsewhere as apple Charlotte or apple brown betty. There are many variations of apple cakes, crumbles, puddings, cobblers, crisps, and pandowdies.

A traditional English recipe which has taken many forms over the centuries is Apply Moyse. One variation calls for the boiling of a dozen apples, which are then strained after they are reduced to a pulp. Three or four egg yolks are then added to the pulp along with rose water, sweet butter, and sugar. The mixture is boiled and eaten with biscuits, cinnamon and ginger.

Several traditional apple dessert recipes do not involve cooking the apples. The British make toffee apples, in which fresh apples are dipped in toffee and allowed to cool before eating. Similarly, the American candy apple and caramel apple are made with different coatings. The Jewish celebration of the New Year—Rosh Hashanah—includes eating apples with honey to invoke the sweetness of the coming year.

Many apple recipes seek to preserve the fruit for the winter, or even further into the future. The most basic is apple butter. The fruits are boiled very slowly without added sugar. They form into a very thick, brown, sweet substance which holds indefinitely.

A straightforward apple marmalade can be made by peeling, coring, and chopping twelve pounds of apples and combining these with six pounds of sugar and one quart of apple cider. This is simmered until the apples are soft. The concoction is then strained and stored in jars.

To produce apple jelly, quarter six pounds of any kind of apple in a preserving pan with a lemon. Cover and boil until the apples become pulp. Strain through cloth overnight. Return juice to pan with addition of one pound of sugar for every pint of juice. Boil this combination for 45 minutes or until the jelly sets. Store in jars.

Breakfast tray with apple sauce, yogurt and pinoli and an apple danish.

OPPOSITE: *Decorative crabapple branches in a vase.*

ABOVE: *Apple decoration on a buffet table.*

A dessert of Apple blintzes.

A variation of apple jelly can be made with crabapples. The fruit is first boiled with six cloves and an inch of ginger until it turns to pulp. After straining, the liquid is mixed with 3/4 of a pound of sugar for every pint of juice and boiled until it jells.

In several recipes similar to those for jelly, apples are preserved with ginger. Four pounds of sugar are boiled into a syrup with three pints of water. Add two ounces of essence of ginger and four pounds of apples, peeled and cored; boil until the apples become transparent. Store the mixture in jars. Alternatively, cut three pounds of apples into small pieces and soak in water with one-quarter pound of crystallized ginger. Meanwhile, boil the cores and peels of these apples with water in a pan until soft. Strain the mixture, measure the liquid, and return it to the pan. For every three pints of juice, add two pounds of sugar. Drain and weigh the apples that have been soaking with the ginger. For every three pounds of apple, add two pounds of sugar. The liquid and sugar mixture and the apple, ginger and sugar mixture are then combined in the pan and the whole boiled until soft and then stored in jars.

Apples can also be cooked whole or quartered and then preserved. Spiced apples are made from whole, firm apples. For every three pounds of apples, combine one quart of vinegar, four pounds of sugar, one ounce of cinnamon in stick form, and a half ounce of cloves in a pan and bring to a boil. Add the whole apples and simmer until soft. Remove the apples and place in a jar. Continue to cook the liquid until it becomes a thick syrup. Pour this over the apples. This can be stored for several months in a cool place.

A simpler version of this recipe is to boil six apples gently in just enough water to cover them. When the skin begins to break and the water to turn red, remove the apples, and continue to boil the water, adding sugar and perhaps some clove or lemon peel. When this liquid has reduced, pour it over the apples before storing.

Quartered apples can be boiled with raisins and a small amount of sugar and then preserved. Alternatively, dried apples can be revived by boiling them for forty minutes with raisins or currants and a bit of sugar.

Many apple recipes also address the frugal use of windfall apples, which may be edible although damaged. They are particularly numerous in drought years, and are a hazard, because insects live in them and lay eggs that will produce pests that infest the next year's crop. Windfall apples, after any spoiled parts are cut away, are fine for making a jelly similar to crabapple jelly, being bright red and tart. Apple Fool is another perfect use: After the spoiled parts have been removed, two pounds of apples are cut into chunks without peeling or coring. The chunks are simmered in water with four ounces of brown sugar, and either lemon peel, several cloves, or a cinnamon stick. When the apples are tender, they are put through a sieve and then combined with a cup of cream or custard.

Combining several fruits is another good use of windfalls. Eight pounds each of unpeeled, uncored, quartered apples and pears can be combined with eight pounds of whole plums and a quarter ounce of cloves and simmered until soft in just enough water to cover the bottom of the pan. Strain the pulp through a very fine sieve, return it to the pan to boil until the liquid becomes a thick syrup. Store in jars.

Apple chutney is another fine use of apples. About thirty peeled, cleaned, cored, and sliced apples are put in a pan with 3/4 of a pound of brown sugar and one quart of vinegar. Cook until tender and then let cool. To this cooled mixture, add two ounces of salt, four ounces of chopped onion, one clove of chopped garlic, four ounces of raisins, one-half ounce of dried, sliced chilies, one ounce of mustard seed, and three ounces of ginger, which have all been pounded together with mortar and pestle. Store in jars.

There are, of course, many ways to enjoy raw apples, from frozen apple cubes for hot days to slices with cheese as a snack; also in sandwiches and salads. Apple sandwiches can be made with bread and butter and sliced apples, or apples, cheese, and horseradish in a grilled sandwich. Salads can be made with spinach, raisin, and apple slices with a dressing of lemon juice, olive oil, and cider vinegar. A Waldorf salad is made of chopped fresh, crisp apples combined with sliced celery and chopped walnuts in a dressing of mayonnaise, lemon juice and honey.

APPLE DRINKS

A final, major category of apple consumption is drinks. Hard cider is today's main commercial use of apples. France, especially Normandy, produces a lot of apple cider, as does the west of England and the Basque region of Spain. Stronger alcoholic versions of apple drinks are Calvados and applejack.[**] The greatest apple drink is Calvados, also one of the best spirits of any description. A.J. Liebling describes a Paris restaurateur, Monsieur Pierre, from Arranches, across from Mont-Saint-Michel, who "sometimes spends weekends calling on peasants in his automobile and trying to wheedle from them a few bottles or—wild dream—a small keg of the veritable elixir of Eden. (Every Norman knows that the apple of the Bible is symbolic; it stands for the distilled cider that will turn the head of any woman.) Good Calvados is never sold legally. The tax leaves a taste that the Normans find intolerable, like the stuff that wives put in whiskey to cure alcoholics." Apple juice is also a popular product, as are cider vinegar and verjuice, related in use to vinegar, but usually made from crabapples.

Every farm once produced its own apple cider each autumn in a days-long process. Apples are collected and placed on the floor of the pound house, which contains the pounder, the press, and the vats. The pounder crushes the apples by running them between two rollers with teeth. One man turns its handle while another pours the fruit in at the top. The resulting pulp and juice then go in capacious shovels from the pounder to the press, which has a large high-sided tray at the lowest level, tipped slightly toward a lip at the front. The pulp is placed on the tray of the press in alternate layers with straw. These alternating layers combine to make the "cheese." At the top of the press is a large wooden screw. When the cheese has been prepared and stands a yard or more in height in the tray, the screw is turned and the pressing begins. Vats placed at the lip of the tray catch the pressed-out juice. The cider is stored for a month or two before it is "hard" and ready to drink.

The production of cider is now especially encouraged in the west of England, where it has a long tradition. Competitions and awards encourage its preservation and development.

Many apple drinks can be produced domestically. Spiced cider is made by adding a half teaspoon of allspice, one teaspoon of cloves, and one cinnamon stick to a quart of cider and simmering gently. Variations can be made by adding other juices—orange or pineapple—or adding brown sugar, ginger, or raisins.

To make an apple and egg cream, a single apple can be boiled and then put through a sieve. After the pulp has cooled, it can be combined with a beaten egg white and cream.

Unfiltered cloudy apple juice, containing crushed bits of peel, is usually best. I love the Apfelsaft sold in Austria, and can offer an excellent way to counter the wasps that buzz around hoping to share your Linzertorte in an outdoor café. Just leave a little liquid in the bottom of the Apfelsaft bottle and put it to one side. The wasps fly into the bottle and, delighted with the juice, become too confused to climb back out. They fly around and around inside and leave you alone.

[**] That very grand figure, Richard Whitney, our immediate neighbor on 73rd Street when I was a boy, became intoxicated by an applejack *stock*, rather than the booze itself. He poured his own money, his firm's and its clients' money, that of the Stock Exchange, of which he was treasurer, and likewise that of the New York Yacht Club, into the stock, which went down, down, down. He was sent to Sing Sing. For an account of this distressing episode see my *Famous Financial Fiascos*, which will immunize you against similar follies.

Tray with fresh apple cider and bread. BELOW: *A tray with Calvados and cookies.*

Varieties

There are thousands of varieties of apples. New ones constantly arise accidentally, but over time they become concentrated in the most commercially interesting. Here are some of the major ones.

Red Delicious: It has a bright red color and a mild, sweet flavor considered by some to be insipid, as it lacks acid, like tangerine juice compared to orange juice. Crunchy, and elongated in shape, with five knobs on the bottom, it is America's favorite. It originated in 1872 as an accidental seedling on the Iowa farm of Jess Hiatt, who sold it as Hiatt's Hawkeye. Then Stark Brothers, a large fruit company, bought the farm and renamed the variety Delicious. From the Red Delicious others have been developed, such as the Starking (or sometimes Star King), the main apple produced in Washington State.

Golden Delicious: Pale green in color, ripening to yellow. Speckled with a faint red flush. It has a crisp flesh, which becomes limp when stored overlong. It ends in five knobs at the bottom. The white flesh does not brown readily. It grew from an accidental seedling on a farm in West Virginia about 1900, and is now widely diffused. The flavor and texture varies according to the location: In cooler areas more acidity is formed, avoiding the bland flavor resulting in warmer areas. It is not actually related to the Red Delicious. The similar name is because the same firm owns both varieties. It is good in salads and for baking, both because it retains its shape and because the peel is so tender that the fruit rarely needs to be peeled before cooking.

McIntosh: It is red, tart, juicy and soft, and crisp. It was first discovered as an accidental seedling by John McIntosh in 1811 in East Ontario, Canada, and is considered the national apple of Canada. It is the major product of New York State apple growers, and is particularly good for applesauce. The **Macoun** variety, which was bred from the McIntosh, has a better flavor and keeps longer.

Granny Smith: Even fully ripe it is bright green. It has a tart flavor with a hint of almond, and firm, juicy flesh. It originated in the late 19th century when an Australian, Maria Ana Smith, who had emigrated from Sussex, grew the seedlings which had sprouted in her yard from some discarded French crabapples. They thrived, and her two sons-in-law, both professional apple farmers, grew them very successfully. This variety came back to Britain, and is now widely grown in such warm climates as Australia, Chile, France, and South Africa. It is good for cooking and baking, which enhances the tartness.

Rome Beauty: Dark red in color, it has pungent, rather mealy flesh. It grew from a stray seedling found by Joel Gillett on his Ohio farm about 1820. An apple tree onto which he had grafted a branch grew another branch below the graft, which began to produce solid red apples. It is particularly good for baking, because it retains its shape, and the cooking enriches the flavor.

Winesap: This variety is dark red, tending toward violet. Juicy and fragrant, it has been much favored by makers of non-alcoholic cider in New Jersey since the early 1800s because of its spicy, almost wine-like flavor. It stores well.

Newtown Pippin: Yellow-green, crisp flesh and a good, tart flavor. It was first grown on Long Island in the 1700s. Benjamin Franklin took samples to England, where they became very popular. It is returning to the U.S., although the trees are described as awkward to manage. Stores well.

Red Delicious

Golden Delicious

McIntosh

Granny Smith

Greening Apples

64

Macoun (above) and **Winesap** (right)

Gala: Yellow with red highlights, heart-shaped, from New Zealand. It is sweet, good for eating in applesauce and salads, and for baking.

Fuji: The color ranges from yellow-green to orange. The taste is mild, spicy, and sweet with crisp flesh. It was developed in Japan as a cross between the Red Delicious and the Ralls Janet. Already the most popular apple in Japan, it is gaining in popularity in the U.S. Storage improves its flavor.

Jonagold: A cross between the Jonathan and the Golden Delicious, it has a tangy sweet flavor, with crisp flesh, and is good for both eating and cooking.

Mutsu (also known as Crispin and Honey Crisp): Developed in Japan from the Golden Delicious.

Empire: McIntosh/Red Delicious crossed in Geneva, New York 1966. Dark red with heavy, waxy bloom. Moderately subacid flesh. High dessert quality, also good for cider.

Stayman: Bright red in color, it has a full flavor and fragrant, crisp flesh. It developed as a sucker on a Winesap tree. Fine for cooking, it stores well.

Criterion: Yellow with a red blush, with a juicy, sweet flavor. Its white flesh does not brown readily.

Arkansas Black: A remarkably deep red in color, almost black. Very hard, the flesh is both sweet and tart. It stores very well.

Braeburn: It varies from green-gold with red in sections to almost all red. Its strong flavor combines sweet and tart. The crisp flesh is aromatic. It was discovered as an accidental seedling in 1952 near Nelson, New Zealand, probably as a cross between a Lady Hamilton and a Granny Smith.

Gala

Mutsu or Crispin

Fuji, Jonagold, Empire, and Matsu

Braeburn

Lady Apples

SOME SECONDARY VARIETIES

Allington Pippin: It presents a great variety and complexity of flavors as it ages—from bittersweet in November to a pineapple flavor by late December.

Api (Pomme d'Api) or **Lady Apple**: This variety dates from Roman times. It is a small, hard winter apple with good flavor, mostly in the skin.

Bismarck: A bright red apple, which is unusual in England. Developed in Tasmania, it was introduced to Britain in 1890s.

Blenheim Orange: Dull yellow and red, of unusually large size, with crisp flesh and an unusually acid flavor. It is considered one of the best members of the Pippin family. Since it ripens in December, it is a traditional Christmas apple.

Bramley's Seedling: Green, sometimes with faint red stripes, it will turn yellow if allowed to remain on the tree. Large with an irregular shape, it stores well, and is the most popular cooking apple in Britain.

Calville blanc: Golden in color, large, juicy and fragrant: of French origin.

Pomme Grise: Particularly good for cooking and pies.

Wickson: Named after the California pomologist, it is said to make wonderful champagne cider.

Cortland: Yellow and red, quite large, with a sweet, moderately acid flavor. It was bred in the U.S. from Ben Davis and McIntosh.

Wickson, Calville blanc and **Pomme Grise apples.**

Costard: The first important kitchen apple, it was also one of the first to have a specific name, which was already in use in England in the 1200. It began to disappear toward the end of the 1600s, and is now extinct. It survives in the word costermonger, as a name for a seller of any fruit or vegetable, usually from a barrow. This name is unrelated to Dutch Koster or Coster, a church officer.

Cort pendu plat: Green with faint red stripes, it may have been developed in Roman times.

Cox's Orange Pippin: Dull brownish-green with faint red stripes and a red blush on one side, this is considered the best of the Pippin family. It was introduced in Great Britain in early 1800, and is the most popular British variety. Alas, the grave of Richard Cox, propagator of Cox's Pippin, is due to be obliterated by the extension of Terminal Five at Heathrow Airport.

Discovery: Bright green and crimson, with a flavor suggesting raspberry. The name arises from its chance discovery by an amateur. It has been marketed widely since the 1970s.

Elstar (or **Lustre Elstar**): Dutch cross of Golden Delicious and Ingrid Marie. Harvest in late August and has large fruit with firm flesh. Very good for fresh eating and cooking. Flavor increases with about four weeks storage.

Ellison's Orange: It tastes of aniseed and pear drops.

Faro: A large, juicy, sweet and acidic fruit. French, from the Brie area, it was identified by the 1300s, and is used in *tarte tatin*.

Flower of Kent: This may have been the apple that supposedly inspired Isaac Newton's ideas about gravitation.

Gillyflower: Fragrant and flavorful, it is mentioned by early writers.

Gladstone: A large early summer apple.

Gravenstein: Yellow with bright stripes of red and orange, and a large, peculiar shape. It was developed in Northern Germany or Denmark before 1800, and brought to California in the 1820s, where it found favor for eating and cooking.

Greening (or **Rhode Island Greening**): Pale green, it was grown from seed by a Mr. Green in Green's End, Rhode Island.

Idared (or Ida Red): Red and yellow, of medium size, having a sweet flavor with some acidity. It was developed in the 1940s from the Jonathan and Wagener varieties, and is popular in England.

James Grieve: A pleasant dessert apple.

Laxton: A large group of apples that can be traced to the horticulturist Thomas Laxton (1830–1890). With his sons, he crossbred many highly successful cultivars that are the forebears of such British dessert apples as Laxton's Pearmain, Laxton's Superb, and Laxton's Fortune.

Elstar

Northern Spy: A yellow and red striped American apple, loved by both country and city people.

Pearmain: This is the oldest recorded English apple name, found in a document of 1204 from Norfolk. The best known variety is the Worcester Pearmain. It has a sharp flavor with a hint of strawberry.

Pippin: This word is derived from the French *pepin*, meaning both the seed and the apple. It originally referred to any apple grown from a pip. In the 1500s, the word was used for any hard, acidic, late-ripening, long-keeping apples. More recent times have brought the Ribston Pippin and from it, the Cox's Orange Pippin. The Sturmer Pippin is grown in the southern locations of South Africa and Australia.

Reinette: Originally, any apple grown by grafting. The word is derived from Latin "renatus" meaning reborn. It soon came to describe apples which were dull green in skin with frequent russeting and occasional flushes of red. Particular varieties are the Golden Reinette, which was known and popular in France before 1650, and the Orleans Reinette, which was developed in the 1700s and has a notably sweet flavor.

Champagne Reinette (above) and **Canada Reinette**

Russet: This term refers to a group of apples with matte brown skin, frequently spotted or flushed red, a flat or lopsided shape, and crisp flesh with a pearlike flavor. The size varies. In England, Egremont Russet and Golden Russet are the most popular, while in Europe the Royal Russet is favored for cooking. An American version, the Roxbury Russet, apparently was developed in Roxbury, Massachusetts in the early 1600s. If true, this would make it America's oldest named variety.

Wealthy: Bright red, with a sharp flavor, it was developed in the 1860s by Peter Gideon, the first scientific American breeder. This apple grows well in northern locations, which was his aim. It's named for his wife, who bore the Puritan name of Wealthy Gideon.

White Joaneting: This shiny yellow English apple ripens in July, before any other.

White Transparent: Very pale with a transparent skin, it was developed in Russia or Scandinavia and introduced to England and the U.S. in the mid-1800s. The Yellow Transparent is similar.

The **Wild Apple (Malus sylvestris)**: Native to Europe and Western Asia, it has a short trunk, but can reach 40 feet in height. It blooms in spring, while the fruit ripens in summer, and when cut crosswise reveals the pentagram so important to Druid and Witch rituals. It is not cultivated in China, where instead there are wild crabapples as well as the cherry-apple. (For the Chinese the blossom symbolizes female beauty.)

York Imperial: It has a patchy color, and a large, lopsided shape, which makes it popular. It stores well, and is favored for processing, rather than retail sale

Quince

A fragrant cousin of the pear and the apple, originally from Southwest Asia. The strongly perfumed flesh is good for cooking apple sauce and jelly.

ABOVE AND OPPOSITE: *Blossoming Quince tree.*
LEFT: *Quince fruit in basket.*

CRABAPPLE

Native to the British Isles, the tree is rarely taller than 25 feet. Its bark is gnarled; it has thorns, unlike cultivars. The scent resembles honeysuckle, and is very attractive to bees, so it is often planted in orchards to help with pollination.

For an idea of the natural process of creating new cultivars, consider the happenstance of the crabapple that happened to fall into the hollow trunk of a chestnut tree and grow there. This was in the hillside village of Caralini, above Città di Castello in Umbria. To the farmer's surprise and gratification the resulting fruits were large and of excellent quality, with a light chestnut aroma. The skin was a handsome green, which became somewhat yellow as it matured. But the particular merit of this chestnut-apple was its durability. Harvested in October, it is still delicious at Eastertide, late in March ("Just as long as the mice don't eat them," said Auplo, the farmer), and often into May. The wonder of nature!

Incidentally, the crabapple has a valuable use unrelated to human consumption, namely as a hedge. For centuries it found favor in England for this purpose.

APPLE COLLECTIONS

In the County of Kent, England, the Brogdale Horticultural Trust is the home of the National Fruit Collection. On 150 acres, it includes more than 2,300 varieties of apple, 550 of pear, 350 of plum, 220 of cherry, and 320 of bush fruits, as well as collections of vines and nuts. The Trust has built up a vast collection of apples, some dating to Roman times. Ever since then, Kent has long been a center of fruit growing in England. Richard Harris, Fruitier to Henry VIII, developed England's first large orchard in Teynham, only a few miles distant. He sought varieties worldwide. For the next three centuries, Kent supplied luxuries to London.

In 1991, the British Ministry of Agriculture, Fisheries and Food offered the Brogdale orchard for sale. Prince Charles believed that the genetic material that it contained should not be put at risk, and so provided funds to buy the land and collections. In due course the Brogdale Horticultural Trust gave its collection of apples to Prince Charles' estate at Highgrove.

The world's largest collection of apples is at the U.S. Department of Agriculture's Plant Genetic Resources Unit, part of which is housed on a 50-acre farm kept up by Cornell University in Geneva, New York. The Department of Agriculture maintains genetic plant collections to be able to strengthen weaknesses found in cultivated varieties. Plants of all types are susceptible to the rigors of the natural world—drought, disease, insects, flooding, temperature changes—but the hope is that cross-breeding cultivated or wild species can create stronger plants with desirable characteristics.

The Department of Agriculture's collection includes live trees, seeds, and cuttings, frozen at minus 300 degrees. Horticulturist Philip L. Forsline, who has been the curator of the apple collection since 1984, has made several trips to central Asia, including the Tian Shan mountains in Kazakhstan, where the apple originated and where the forbears of current domestic apples live in the wild. Some of these trees are over 300 years old. Through his expeditions, Forsline was able to add 140,000 seeds and 900 cuttings of the apple's wild relatives to the collection.

Currently, about 2,500 varieties of cultivated and wild apples grow on the farm in Geneva, New York. Horticulturists are cataloguing the apples in the collection to permit exact breeding for desirable qualities. Four years are needed before one can taste the results of a cross-breeding attempt. The next step will be to hire geneticists to examine the apple more minutely, so that cross-breeding can be done scientifically.

An apple breeding program involving Purdue, Rutgers, and the University of Illinois has produced a variety of flavorful and disease-resistant varieties, including Prima, Priscilla, Priam, Sir Prize, Jonafree, Redfree, Dayton, William's Pride, and McShay.

Apple orchard, Glynwood Farm, Cold Spring, New York.
Photograph by Maria Bonsanti

GROWING APPLES

The apple exists in thousands of varieties, called cultivars, an elision of the words "cultivated variety." Botanically, it is a member of the rose family, and appropriately, the blossom is very fragrant.

Only a very small percentage of the extant apple cultivars are grown commercially. In 2005, more than 55 million tons were grown worldwide, worth about $10 billion. The largest producer, China, produced 40% of this total, putting tremendous pressure on the market in the U.S. The United States came in second, with 7.5%. Other major producers are Turkey, France, Italy and Iran.

The annual American apple harvest is roughly 10 billion pounds, divided among 35 states. Washington State produces the most bountiful harvest, 4.3 billion pounds, and New York follows with one billion. Other significant contributors are Michigan, with 930 million pounds, California, with 800 million, Pennsylvania/West Virginia/Maryland, with 792 million, Maine/New Hampshire, with 135 million, Utah/Colorado, with 130 million, and Missouri/Illinois, with 110 million.

The commercial harvest is comprised of only 20 different varieties, and 80% of this production is made up of only eight varieties, Red Delicious, Golden Delicious, Granny Smith, McIntosh, Rome Beauty, Jonathan, York, and Stayman. Granny Smith only recently climbed past McIntosh to third place.

A list of favorite varieties from a century back would include many apples now rarely seen. Back then, more than 700 varieties were grown just in New York State. Commercial apple production concentrates on those varieties with desired characteristics of appearance, uniform size, hardiness for travel, and large yield. Because the trees are long-lived, however, older varieties that are no longer commercially cultivated can be recaptured from the remains of abandoned orchards by taking scions or pips.

Although commercial apple production supports only a handful among the huge range of apple cultivars, increasing numbers of farmers and home gardeners grow heirloom varieties. Local agricultural extension services offer advice, and growers exchange scions. Farmers' markets offer local varieties specific to their localities. Apple conservation groups have been formed to support their growth and sale to prevent their extinction.

A viable commercial apple must be both soft and crisp. The color must be appealing and fairly regular, without russeting. The shape should resemble that of the Red Delicious. It must resist disease, and have a long stem. The tree must bear a large quantity of fruit, which must be able to tolerate long storage times and withstand shipment. And of course, the flavor must be pleasing!

Apple orchard in bloom, Trentino region, Italy.

Many cultivars that are delicious to eat, sometimes better than the most heavily produced varieties, never enter commercial production because they lack other necessary qualities. They may have an irregular or odd shape, be russeted, prone to disease, produce a small yield, or be intolerant of storage or shipment. However, some cultivars are so prized that they are grown commercially in quantity despite problems. In England, Cox's Orange Pippin and the Egremont Russett are widely grown although prone to disease.

Tastes vary over time. The currently dominant cultivars are sweeter than many older ones. Although most Americans and Europeans prefer a sweet (subacid) apple, some like them tarter. Washington State's famous Delicious is losing favor with some apple fanciers because of its mild flavor and relatively soft texture. Very sweet apples (almost without acid) are preferred in Asia, particularly in India.

Most cultivars have been developed to be eaten fresh. These are called dessert apples. In some areas of the world, particularly England, cooking apples are a separate category, but frequently they overlap. A third category is the cider apple. Apples bred for hard cider are too bitter to eat fresh, but they give the drink a richer flavor than would dessert apples.

Apple trees that are grown from seeds, intentionally or spontaneously, are very different from the trees that originally produced those seeds. Spontaneous variations can also develop when apple trees produce "bud sports," mutations directly on the tree. Sometimes these bud sport mutations can be improvements on the original cultivar, and even be distinctive enough to become a new cultivar. Most cultivars are developed by careful crossbreeding of different varieties with desirable characteristics. Some have been crossbred successfully with crabapple trees in order to produce hardier cultivars. The climate of Minnesota has encouraged such propagation, carried out at the Excelsior Experiment Station at the University of Minnesota. Since the 1930s, breeding has produced such successful hardy cultivars as the Haralson, Wealthy, Honeygold, and Honeycrisp.

Apple trees are usually produced by grafting scions of the desired cultivar onto an appropriate rootstock. First, one produces the rootstock, either from a seedling or from cloning. After a year, the branches of the rootstock seedling are cut away and replaced with a scion—a small piece of branch of the desired cultivar. The rootstock and the scion grow together over time to result in a tree of the desired type.

Apple orchards Trentino region, Italy.

Apple blossoms in Morocco.

Apple blossoms in Tuscany.

Apple orchard with protective netting, Trentino region, Italy.

Cato, in *De Agricultura*, describes how he grafts. "Cut the end of the branch you are going to graft, slope it a bit so that the water will run off, being careful not to tear the bark. Get a hard stick and sharpen the end. Mix clay or chalk, a little sand, and cattle dung, and knead them together to make a sticky mass. Drive the sharpened stick between the bark and the wood two fingertips deep. Then take the scion, and sharpen the end obliquely for a distance of two fingertips; take out the dry stick that you have just driven in and drive in the shoot you want to graft. Fit bark to bark, and drive it in to the end of the slope. You can graft a second, a third, and a fourth shoot. Smear the join with the kneaded mixture, and cover the whole, so that if it rains the water will not soak into the bark. Finally, wrap it in straw and bind tightly, to keep the cold from injuring it."

Although the choice of rootstock does not determine the resulting cultivar, it will determine some of its characteristics. Commercial apple growers can select from among a wide range of rootstock options, but home gardeners usually have only two, the standard rootstock, which produces a full-size tree, or the semi-dwarf rootstock, which produces a somewhat smaller one. Dwarf rootstocks are slightly less hardy, more likely to suffer wind or cold damage.

American commercial apple growers seem to be planting more dwarf trees than formerly. These grow best if supported by trellises or posts. They mature in five or six years. Orchards of dwarf apple trees have historically been more common in Europe than America. The trees are about ten feet high, rather than thirty, although the apples are the usual full size. The fruit is much more easily harvested, with less chance of damage. In addition, because many more dwarf trees than full-sized trees can be planted on the same acreage, the yield from the same plot may increase.

In order to establish an orchard, two to four-year-old trees are grown in a nursery, grafted onto rootstock, and then planted outdoors. They will grow in nearly any soil as long as it is well drained. They should be planted in locations not prone to early spring frosts, and not on south-facing slopes in the northern hemisphere or north-facing slopes in the southern hemisphere. Those positions encourage early spring flowering, which makes the trees susceptible to spring frosts.

Good air flow around the trees is important, so while a location on a slope is desirable, it should not be a slope that encourages blooming in early spring when frost is still possible. Some like a location near water, which can retard warming when frost is likely, such as the eastern shore of Lake Michigan, the southern shore of Lake Ontario, and near other lakes. However, those areas also have cool, humid spring weather, which encourages fungal growth. The very best areas for apple growing mimic the climate where it first grew, such as northern China, central Turkey, and eastern Washington State, and at a distance from water, with cold winters followed by short, warm springs having little chance of frost.

Clockwise from above, apple picking, apples being loaded into a bin, apples being hauled out of the orchard. Trentino region, Italy.

Once the trees are planted outdoors in a favorable location, standard trees grow for five to ten years before bearing fruit, and semi-dwarf for three to five. During this period the trees must be tended carefully to develop a sturdy frame to bear the weight of the fruit. Limbs should be trained in the proper direction and pruned to admit light. Buds heading in the wrong locations should be nipped.

To bear fruit, apple trees must be cross-pollinated, so there should be nearby pollenizers, such as other apple or crabapple trees, with enough compatible pollen to do the job. Nurseries can provide a list of which trees provide compatible pollen. Orchards solve this problem by planting alternating rows of compatible cultivars, or planting occasional crabapples throughout the orchard, or grafting crabapple branches onto apple trees. This practice can be implemented on a smaller scale by placing large bouquets of crabapple branches near apple trees.

Then, you need bees. You can put hives in the orchard. It takes many visits from the bees to pollinate successfully. A late frost, after the trees have bloomed, can fatally interrupt the pollination process...a reason not to plant the trees on warm slopes where there's a risk of blooming during a frost. A severe enough frost will damage the flower, and no fruit will be produced.

Successful pollination results in good quality apples with between seven and ten seeds. Fewer than three seeds, and the fruit may drop early in the summer.

The production from a single apple tree can vary greatly from year to year. A mature standard tree can produce up to 500 kilos of apples annually, and a dwarf tree produces 10 to 80 kilos. Apples tend to bear fruit in a two-year cycle: years of very high yield followed by little or almost none. This cycle can be evened out by thinning in the plentiful years when the trees are in bloom to encourage better production in the following one. Commercial orchards think chemically, not a practical approach for home growers. Apple blossoms occur in groups of five, or occasionally six. The first one to bloom is called the "king bloom." It has the best chance of developing into a well-formed fruit. The king bloom tends to suppress the development of the four or five other blooms of its group. If they appear nevertheless, they should be removed.

After the blooms are set and pollinated and the fruit is ready to develop, hazards remain, such as fungal and bacterial diseases, insects and mammalian pests. The nastiest fungal diseases are gymnosporangium rust, apple scab, and black spot. The most serious bacterial disease is fireblight. The plum curculio is the worst insect, followed by the apple maggot and the coddling moth. Mice eat the bark of young trees, deer eat the shoots.

Spraying the trees with kaolin clay holds down the pests. Commercial orchards spray regularly, although not while the trees are blooming, for fear of killing the necessary pollinators. All these pests make organic apple growing difficult. Successful orchards plant disease-resistant cultivars.

Cider Apples: English. Extremely bitter, this use of cider refers only to the fermented beverage. The American use of the word cider usually refers to unfermented apple juice, not these apples.

Apple cider is classified according to the acidity and tannin levels of the apples used in production. "Sharp" implies high acidity and low tannin, "bittersweet" suggests low acidity and higher tannin levels. Some of the apples used for each are the following:

Sharp: **The Frederick apple**.

Bitter-sharp: **The Kingston Black** and **Stoke Red**.

Bittersweet: **The Yarlington Mill**, **Dabinet** and **Hangdown**.

Sweet: The **Court Royal**, **McIntosh**, **Red Delicious**, **Golden Delicious**, **Rome**, **Winesap** and **Sweet Coppin**.

The County of Somerset in Great Britain is particularly rich in apples. Glastonbury was known in earlier centuries as Avallon, meaning the isle of apples. Over 150 varieties of apples can be traced to that county, which is still a center both for orchards and the production of apple cider and apple wine.

OPPOSITE TOP: *McIntosh tree, New Jersey.*
ABOVE: *Cider press.* RIGHT: *a variety of apples for pressing.* BELOW: *leftover pulp.*

The final step is from the tree to the market. You pick apples using three-legged ladders placed among the branches. Michigan State University engineers are developing an electronic device that will travel with the fruit and record the journey in order to make it less harmful. The device is embedded in a beeswax sphere, 3½ inches in diameter. Inside the sphere are a battery, an accelerometer to measure bumps, a microprocessor that shows the bumps that bruise the apples, and a clock to record when those bumps happened. Once this information has been processed by a computer, you can find the bumps, grade the path, and give the apples a smoother journey on their way to market.

BELOW: *Early 20th century engraving of cider pressing.*

OPPOSITE: *Photo depicting old ways of transporting and pressing apples.*

MAKING CIDER

The best cider in America is Farnum Hill, from Lebanon, New Hampshire. Here's what the *New York Times* says about it: "Farnum Hill's ciders stand alone. If you swirl a glass of the sparkling semidry, a waft of citrus blossoms and pear travels up to your nose. It is dry and crisp, with a gentle warming quality, like a Scotch. Steven and Louisa Wood blend up to a dozen rare varieties of apples like Esopus Spitzenberg, Dabinett, Yarlington Mill, Kingston Black and Médaille d'Or. Their extra dry has the same kind of vibrancy, with an aroma of cherries and melon that seems to leap from the glass. It is dry and distinct with a pleasant sharpness reminiscent of better oranges. Both would be terrific with a meal."

Barrels for Cider.

In olden times, water was often septic, so people drank more beer, wine, and hard cider. In fact the word cider meant hard cider, as it still does in England and France. Colonial America consumed enormous quantities. John Adams downed a tankard with breakfast. Then came the 18th Amendment, meaning the end of the alcoholic content. Real (hard) cider no more resembles apple juice, the unfermented version, than grape juice resembles wine. But real cider, three to eight percent alcohol, is making a brisk comeback, and is starting to compete with wine and beer.

As a former wine chateau proprietor myself (in the Médoc) I recognize much of the process that Steven Wood follows to make his superb product.

You let the fruit ripen until it is rich in sugar, the source of the alcohol. In the wine business the picked grapes go straight to the fermentation vat. Apples, though, are picked by hand and placed in bins to be conveyed to the grinder, where they are turned into pulp, which resembles applesauce, and is called pomace. It is folded into stout cloths and stacked on racks to be squeezed. Then, in cloth bundles, it moves on to a hydraulic press, from which pours the fresh juice, full and spicy. The next step is blending the juices of different varieties and sending the mixture to ferment in vats and barrels. This unpasteurized juice contains wild yeasts that stimulate the fermentation, just as in winemaking; and again as with wine, you can add special yeasts for particular flavors, or add sugar to lift the alcohol level.

At Farnum Hill the juices ferment slowly with the help of a cold-hardy champagne yeast, chosen for its lack of flavor signature. Like wine, cider is aged in the barrel, very briefly for most ciders, and a year or two for Farnum Hill. Then it goes to the market, to bring a good price, one hopes.

The apple grower's year runs in a laborious cycle. Pruning goes on throughout winter and early spring. Then, when the trees emerge from dormancy, a short grafting period opens: you can replace less desired varieties with preferred ones by cutting off whole tops and inserting pencil sized scions into the stumps. When the ground firms up, a tractor-mounted brush chopper moves through each aisle, shredding pruned-off branches into the soil and opening the way for later tractor work. With luck, in the weeks before bloom, you can sometimes stall the fungal, viral and insect pests. During the bloom, one aids pollination by introducing bees, which means renting hives. Honeybees avoid cold, wind, or rain. They must all be returned to the beekeeper, so you can only apply insecticides, to kill the maggot fly and other pests, at night, when they're back in their hives.

Farm waiting for customers.

After bloom, hail can shred the tiny new fruit. Then follow weeks of mowing, pest monitoring, surveying the various traps and, occasionally spraying. Pocket magnifiers are standard equipment. (One can also introduce ladybugs and the like to feed on the bad bugs.) As always, one is doing maintenance work on equipment. Then pruning gets under way, first with a small chainsaw and then with an eight foot pole clipper.

In late summer you can rest a bit. If you run a fall retail stand, you shift rusty equipment and other eyesores out of view. You welcome fruit-lovers by setting up a big tent or other shopping area.

Then the pickers appear, to work past Halloween. Pressing goes on for weeks after the pickers leave.

In the run-up to Christmas, cider marketing intensifies, following the wine-trade pattern: pouring and tasting in shops, badgering distributors, pursuing press attention. Then follows a "coma," until once more pruning resumes.

And so the farmer's life proceeds, in an endless annual rhythm, and very often an endless sequence of generations, as it has since ancient times.

*An apple orchard in winter,
New Hampshire.*

Fruit garland festooning the entrance of the Palazzo dei Diamanti, Ferrara, Italy.